D0553957

NO LONGER PROPERTY
OF ANYTHINK
RANGEVIEW LIBRARY
DISTRICT

Animal Classifications

Birds

Angela Royston

heinemann raintree

© 2015 Heinemann Raintree
an imprint of Capstone Global Library, LLC
Chicago, Illinois

To contact Capstone Global Library, please call
800-747-4992, or visit our web site www.capstonepub.com

All rights reserved. No part of this publication may be
reproduced or transmitted in any form or by any means,
electronic or mechanical, including photocopying,
recording, taping, or any information storage and retrieval
system, without permission in writing from the publisher.

Edited by Helen Cox Cannons, Clare Lewis, and
    Abby Colich
Designed by Steve Mead
Picture research by Tracy Cummins
Production by Victoria Fitzgerald
Originated by Capstone Global Library Ltd
Printed and bound in China by Leo Paper Group

18 17 16 15 14
10 9 8 7 6 5 4 3 2 1

Library of Congress Cataloging-in-Publication Data
Royston, Angela, 1945- author.
  Birds / Angela Royston.
    pages cm.—(Animal classification)
  Summary: "This fascinating series takes a very simple
look at animal classifications, with each book focusing on
a different group of animal. This book is about birds: what
they do, how they behave, and how these characteristics
are different from other groups of animals. Beautifully
illustrated with colorful photographs, the book shows
many examples of different types of birds in their natural
environment."—Provided by publisher.
  Includes bibliographical references and index.
  ISBN 978-1-4846-0750-3 (hb)—ISBN 978-1-4846-0757-2
(pb)—ISBN 978-1-4846-0794-7 (ebook) 1. Birds—Juvenile
literature. 2. Animals—Classification—Juvenile literature.
I. Title.

QL676.2.R688 2015
598—dc23   2014013457

**This book has been officially leveled by using the F&P
Text Level Gradient™ Leveling System.**

Acknowledgments
We would like to thank the following for permission to
reproduce photographs: Getty Images: PhotoStock-Israel,
19; Shutterstock: Anneka, 21, anuphadit, 23, Christian
Musat, 15, Dima Fadeev, 5, Dmitry Elagin, 6, efirm, 25, 29
Top, Erni, 12, 29 Bottom, feathercollector, 10, francesco de
marco, 27, Gabriele Maltinti, 8, 28, Gez Alvarez, 18, Jim H
Walling, 4, Karin Jaehne, 24, KellyNelson, 16, ktsdesign,
11, 29 Middle, Cover, Miao Liao, 26, Oldrich, 20, Oleg
Senkov, 7, paula french, 14, PCHT, 22, Stephen Mcsweeny,
9, Sue Robinson, 13, Tabby Mittins, 17, Tracy Starr, Design
Element.

We would like to thank Michael Bright for his invaluable
help in the preparation of this book.

Every effort has been made to contact copyright holders
of material reproduced in this book. Any omissions will
be rectified in subsequent printings if notice is given to
the publisher.

All the Internet addresses (URLs) given in this book were
valid at the time of going to press. However, due to the
dynamic nature of the Internet, some addresses may have
changed, or sites may have changed or ceased to exist since
publication. While the author and publisher regret any
inconvenience this may cause readers, no responsibility for
any such changes can be accepted by either the author or
the publisher.

Contents

Some words are shown in bold, **like this**. You can find out what they mean by looking in the glossary.

Meet the Birds

Owls, hens, penguins, and parrots are all birds. Birds are a group of animals that have wings and **beaks**, and whose bodies are covered with feathers.

Flying allows birds to move quickly from place to place.

Parrots often have very brightly colored feathers.

Scientists sort living things into groups. This is called **classification**. Each group is different from other groups in particular ways. Only birds have feathers.

Body Shape

Birds belong to a bigger group of animals called **vertebrates**. This group includes **mammals** and reptiles. A vertebrate has a **backbone** and a hard **skeleton** inside its body. The skeleton gives the animal its shape.

Pigeons are one of the most common birds in cities around the world.

beak

A flamingo uses its long legs and long neck to stand in water and reach down for food.

Birds come in many different shapes and sizes. All birds have two wings and two legs. Instead of teeth, they have a hard **beak**.

Birds of Prey

Eagles, hawks, and falcons are **birds of prey.** These fierce birds all hunt other animals for food. Some fly high in the air looking for **prey,** such as mice or smaller birds, to catch.

When a falcon spots its prey, it **hovers** above it before diving.

A bird of prey has long, sharp talons.

These birds dive and grab their prey with curved claws called **talons**. They use their curved **beaks** to pull the flesh from their prey.

How Birds Fly

Most birds use their wings to fly through the air. Different birds have different shaped wings. An albatross has huge wings, which allow it to **glide** for thousands of miles.

An albatross's wings measure up to 11 feet (3.5 meters) from wingtip to wingtip.

A hummingbird's wings move so fast they hum!

A hummingbird has tiny wings, which it beats very fast. A hummingbird uses its wings to stay in one place! It **hovers** in the air while it sips sugary **nectar** from flowers.

Champion Fliers

Swifts are champion fliers! They spend most of their lives in the air, and they even sleep as they fly. Their long, curved wings allow them to change direction easily and fly at up to 70 miles (113 kilometers) per hour.

Swifts catch flying insects as they fly through the air.

A peregrine falcon watches its **prey** before it folds its wings and dives to catch it.

A peregrine falcon can move even faster than a swift. When it dives, it can reach 200 miles (320 kilometers) per hour!

Not All Birds Fly!

All birds have wings, but some cannot fly. Ostriches are the biggest birds and are too heavy to fly. Instead, they run fast on their long, strong legs. Roadrunners can fly a little, but they prefer to run!

An ostrich can run at up to 43 miles (70 kilometers) per hour.

Penguins dive underwater to catch fish, squid, and krill to eat.

A penguin cannot fly, but it swims underwater better than any other bird. It uses its wings as **flippers** to pull itself through the water.

Feathers

Birds need strong feathers to fly. Feathers are also useful in other ways. They are waterproof, so they help to keep the bird dry. They trap air close to the skin and keep the bird warm.

A bird uses its **beak** to keep its feathers clean.

This bird is puffing up its feathers to keep itself warm.

Birds are **warm-blooded**, which means they make their own body heat. When they are cold, they puff up their feathers to trap more air, to keep them warmer.

Beaks

The shape of a bird's **beak** is a clue to what it eats. For example, a finch has a strong, short beak, which is good for cracking seeds. Swifts have short, slim beaks for catching insects.

A goldfinch eats the seeds of thistles and other flowers.

Male weaverbirds get their name from the amazing nests they weave.

Birds also use their beaks to carry material, such as twigs and grass, to make a nest. Some birds weave complicated nests with their beaks and feet.

Eggs and Nests

A bird begins life inside an egg, which its mother lays in a nest. The nest might be in a tree or on the ground. Most birds lay several eggs at a time.

Birds' eggs have hard shells, which protect the tiny chicks growing inside.

This duckling has just hatched from its egg.

The mother bird sits on the eggs to keep them warm. When the chicks inside are ready to **hatch,** they break through the shell and struggle out.

Caring for Chicks

As soon as the chicks have **hatched**, the parents begin to feed them. Many chicks eat the same food as their parents. Most chicks stay in the nest and grow bigger. The parents have to work hard to keep them fed!

A sunbird brings food to her young chicks.

This chick is getting ready to fly.

When the young bird's wing feathers have grown, it is ready to fly. Sometimes the parent pushes the bird out of the nest. It soon learns to fly!

Water Birds

Ducks, swans, and some other birds are **classified** as water birds. They can fly through the air, walk on land, and swim in the water. Most have **webbed feet** that help them to swim.

A duck has a large, flat **beak**. Water birds use their beaks to filter the water to find food.

Cygnets stay close to their mother until they can take care of themselves.

Soon after ducklings and **cygnets hatch**, they follow their mother into the water. After a few months, their adult feathers grow and they learn to fly.

One Amazing Bird!

Some birds fly long distances at particular times of the year. This is called **migration**. For example, Canada geese produce their chicks in the **Arctic**, but they migrate south to warmer lands in winter.

Canada geese fly together in a "V" shape when they migrate.

This Arctic tern is resting during its long flight from the North Pole to the South.

No birds fly farther than Arctic terns. Their chicks **hatch** in the Arctic in spring. As the Arctic winter begins, they fly all the way to **Antarctica**! Six months later, they return to the Arctic.

Quiz

Look at the pictures below and read the clues. Can you remember the names of these birds? Look back in the book if you need help.

1. I **hover** in the air until I see my **prey**. Then I dive and catch it. What am I?

Answers
1. falcon
2. swan
3. hummingbird
4. swift

2. I have **webbed feet** and a flat **beak**. What am I?

3. I beat my wings very fast and I feed on **nectar** from flowers. What am I?

4. I fly really fast and I catch insects in midair. What am I?

Glossary

Antarctica large area of frozen land around the South Pole

Arctic area of ocean and land around the North Pole

backbone row of knobby bones in the back

beak hard covering of a bird's mouth

bird of prey bird that hunts other animals for food

classification system that scientists use to divide living things into separate groups

cygnet young swan

flippers flat, bendable parts of the body that animals use to swim

glide move through the air without flapping the wings

hatch break out of an egg

hover stay in one place in the air

mammal one of a group of animals that have hair and feed the young with milk from the mother

migration movement of birds or animals from one place to another and back again

nectar sweet juice found inside flowers

prey animal that is hunted by another animal for food

skeleton hard, bony frame inside the body. It is the skeleton that gives vertebrate animals their shape.

talon long, curved claw

vertebrate animal that has a backbone and skeleton inside its body

warm-blooded able to make body heat from eating food

webbed feet feet that have a layer of skin between the claws

Find Out More

Books

Berger, Melvin and Gilda. *Birds* (True or False). New York: Scholastic, 2010.

Schuetz, Kari. *Birds* (Blastoff!: Animal Classes). Minneapolis: Bellwether, 2013.

Veitch, Catherine. *Bird Babies* (Animal Babies). Chicago: Heinemann Library, 2013.

Web sites

FactHound offers a safe, fun way to find internet sites related to this book. All of the sites on FactHound have been researched by our staff.

Here's all you do:
Visit www.facthound.com
Type in this code: 9781484607503

Index